real baby animals

fuzzy the duckling

by Gisela Buck and Siegfried Buck

For a free color catalog describing Gareth Stevens' list of high-quality books, call 1-800-542-2595 (USA) or 1-800-461-9120 (Canada). Gareth Stevens' Fax: (414) 225-0377.

Library of Congress Cataloging-in-Publication Data available upon request from publisher. Fax: (414) 225-0377 for the attention of the Publishing Records Department.

ISBN 0-8368-1502-5

This North American edition first published in 1996 by
Gareth Stevens Publishing
1555 North RiverCenter Drive, Suite 201
Milwaukee, Wisconsin 53212 USA

This edition first published in 1996 by Gareth Stevens, Inc. Original edition © 1994 by Kinderbuchverlag KBV Luzern (Sauerländer, AG), Aarau, Switzerland, under the title *Watschel das Entenkind*. Translated from the German by John E. Hayes. Adapted by Gareth Stevens, Inc. All additional material supplied for this edition © 1996 by Gareth Stevens, Inc.

Photographer: Othmar Baumli
Watercolor artist: Wolfgang Kill
Series editor: Patricia Lantier-Sampon
Editorial assistants: Diane Laska, Jamie Daniel

Printed in Mexico

1 2 3 4 5 6 7 8 9 99 98 97 96

Gareth Stevens Publishing
MILWAUKEE

One March day, a mother duck
lays eight eggs in her nest.

She sits on the eggs to incubate them.

The eggs have to stay warm. When the duck gets up to eat, she covers the nest with grass and feathers.

After one month, light tapping sounds come from inside the eggs.

Soon, little holes appear.

A small, dark head shows in one egg.

The little head pushes
through and breaks
the shell open.
Something dark and
moist tumbles out.

It's Fuzzy the
duckling. She
is exhausted.

Fuzzy soon lifts her head.

The sun dries her feathers.

A few hours later, Fuzzy is dry and standing up. She wants to leave the nest.

Shortly after all the ducklings
hatch, they waddle down
toward the water.

Mother duck swims away.
Fuzzy is brave. She is the
first to swim to her mother.

Soon, all the ducklings are paddling around their mother. Fuzzy likes to swim in front of everybody.

The ducklings "cheep" excitedly.
Some of them are already
trying to catch tiny animals.

A little farther away, Fuzzy's father
watches over his family.

After a while, they all take a rest in the sun.

Fuzzy helps her mother keep guard.

The young ducks grow quickly.
They are always getting to know
new places on the lake. They
like to hide in the tall grasses.

Two months later, Fuzzy has her adult feathers and can fly. She can live on her own now, and she looks just like her mother.

A young drake with colorful feathers
arrives in the fall. His head is green,
and he has a white neck band.

Fuzzy and the drake become friends.

They like to stay together.

They dive in the water for plants and small animals.

They oil their feathers, so they can stay warm and dry in the water.

One day, another drake
arrives to challenge
Fuzzy's friend.

The two male ducks fight
to see who will mate
with Fuzzy.

The other drake finally gives up.
Fuzzy's friend flaps his wings
because he is glad he won.

The ducks mate in spring.

Then they look for a place to make a nest. There are not many areas on the lakeshore with bushes and grass.

They want to be sure their nest is well protected.

The nest is ready, and
Fuzzy lays her eggs.
If nothing disturbs her
while she sits on them,
her ducklings will hatch
in four weeks.

Further Reading and Videos

All Night Near the Water. Jim Arnosky (Putnam Publishing Group)
Animals At A Glance (4 volumes). (Gareth Stevens)
Arnold of the Ducks. (Playhouse Video)
At the Zoo. (Learning Videos)
Chickens Aren't the Only Ones. (Reading Rainbow Video)
Ducks Don't Get Wet. Augusta Goldin (HarperCollins)
Eyewitness Video: Bird! (Eyewitness Video)
Oliver and the Lucky Duck. Page McBrier (Troll)
Quack and Honk. Allan Fowler (Childrens Press)
The Story About Ping. (Weston Woods Video)
Super Duck: A True Story. Jane S. Williams (Brandylane)
What Hatches From an Egg? Leonardo Binato (Thomasson-Grant)

Fun Facts about Ducks and Ducklings

Did you know . . .

— that ducks and geese fly South for the winter, often traveling distances of over 1,000 miles (1,610 kilometers)?
— that male and female ducks often look very different? The males usually have more colorful feathers than the females.
— that ducks will return year after year to the same place they were hatched to give birth to their own young?
— that baby ducklings and their mothers can recognize each other by the sound of their quacks and calls?
— that, like many other birds, ducks live, travel, and nest in flocks?

Glossary-Index

brave — having courage; not frightened (p. 8).

challenge — to call to a contest in order to determine which is the strongest or best (p. 18).

"cheep" — short, high sound a baby animal makes (p. 10).

disturb — to interrupt (p. 22).

dive — to intentionally go under water, usually head first (p. 17).

drake — a male duck (pp. 15, 16, 18, 19).

exhausted — very tired (p. 5).

hatch — to break out of an egg (pp. 8, 22).

incubate — to keep eggs warm until they hatch (p. 3).

mate — to join together to produce offspring (pp. 18, 20).

moist — damp or slightly wet (p. 5).

nest — a home built by an animal, often as a place where it can give birth and shelter its young (pp. 2, 3, 7, 21, 22).

paddle — to move around in water with broad-sided strokes. For example, a duck paddles through water by swishing its broad, webbed feet (p. 9).

tumble — to roll out; to fall suddenly (p. 5).

waddle — to take short steps with a side-to-side motion (p. 8).